Pain Into purpose

Zoe Cawley

.

Dedication.

To those I've loved and lost to suicide/mental Illness, who will always have a special place in my heart. who I met in the darkest of places but somehow you managed to bring so much light into my life, I can only hope my words, my poetry can bring comfort to a person who is having to fight the same demons that you tried to fight, But could no longer win, ill miss you forever.

And to my support system, the ones I love and care about the most and people I've met along the way from professionals to people in a similar situation to me, to those that love me unconditionally and are one of the reasons I'm still here today. Thank-you. And I forever appreciate you.

Message from the author.

Dear readers,

For those that don't know me personally, I'm Zoe, I am just a girl who turned her pain into poetry and somehow and at some point, poetry turned into my purpose, and this is me publishing my fourth book.
I want my words to be a comfort for someone struggling whether that's knowing someone out there somewhere feels a similar kind of way so they don't have to feel alone or being able to validate what someone is going through and letting them know that their bad thoughts don't make them bad people and showing the world that mental illness is sadly real and affects so many people and people lose their lives to this.
I've lost people to mental illness. I've nearly lost myself. I've seen mental illness take over so many of my loved one's life's.
Ironically, they haven't invented the words to describe just how painful and deliberating mental illness can be, but I tried my very hardest for myself but also for all those that struggle. I wish to spread hope, awareness, understanding and compassion and empathy
And to show the world or at least the individual reading this
That pain really can be turned into purpose! just like i've done,

All my love,

Zoe x

Pain into purpose.

I turned pain into purpose, as I knew if I didn't it would destroy every single part of me,
The pain started to become my identity,
I confined to the fact that being mentally Ill and past memories is just my reality,
Living in constant fight or flight,
Believing it could never get better even if it might,
Losing hope and struggling to cope,
I wanted to be rescued but at same time I wanted people to let me drown,
Constantly feeling on the verge of an emotional breakdown,
A therapist said to me, you've been through things and saw things you were never meant to see,
And I knew I could sit there and let all I've been through destroy me,
But I turned my experience into words and to some people that may not mean much at all,
But sometimes I write the words I wish was said to me back when I was small,
My purpose wasn't found in a subject in school,
No, my purpose was found from my pain,
Putting my experiences in written pieces to help give the words to someone who tries to explain,
what it's like going through the same,
I could let what happened to me eat me alive or I can turn it into a purpose even if it helps me to simply just survive,
Because I never want anyone to feel the way that I did,
I want to validate and have compassion because I never really got any of that as a kid,
The pain that I feel from each and everyday comes out in forms of poetry,
as I try to find the words to something that is so hard to say,
The pain was so much, inside was so easy to destroy,
But despite the pain I've experienced I wish to spread hope and joy
And as wonderful it is to say that despite the dark,
I still have somewhere inside a spark,
That even though I'm sad I can make someone smile,

That even though I've been let down,
for other people I'd go the extra mile,
Pain into purpose,
At the time I didn't know,
That I could use my pain and turn it into something else,
I could watch myself grow,
I love a lot despite being young that's not something I'd regularly receive,
One day you will feel like you are trapped but I promise there will come a day where it starts to feel easier to breathe,
wait for that day, choose to stay,
Because pain doesn't define who you are,
Or stop you from going far,
I found a purpose in my pain,
and I promise you there's going to be a day where you can find the same.

Where wealth is found.

Society tends to describe being rich based on materialistic objects,
currency or pounds,
But I believe the term 'being rich' is much more profound,
Of course, money is important we need it in order to survive,
But having less than some,
doesn't mean the working class or lower class can't thrive,
It's always who's got the best toy?
not who has felt the most joy,
Because sometimes it doesn't take a lot,
there can be beauty in finding satisfaction in what we have got,
I got told I should be grateful for everything I got as a kid,
I got food, I got a roof over my head,
To me it was said,
You have had a lot, a lot more than other kids did,
I'm sorry,
I don't mean to be ungrateful, and this is nothing to do with greed,
I say I just don't think that meets a child's internal needs,
Being nurturing and affectionate,
It's a definite,
That these are the things most valuable for a child's development,
Wealth and being rich can have many definitions,
It's just what we choose to see,
What part of it is internal or external that is making us happy?
A kid could go home to a big mansion,
with all that he could ever ask for,
His friends at school maybe jealous and says `well he has it all,`
But if he goes home to no love or affection,
Then it doesn't matter about the materialistic things that seems cool,
The only joy he's gets is from a fancy toy,
While he looks out the window,
And he sees another boy,
with a simple hug from the mother,
The love and care that radiates off one another,
The thing that kids in school didn't understand,
is the thing with the most value isn't what's in that little boy's hand,
Because to everyone else,

he was lucky he has a lot,
But really the little boy said to himself without love and care what have I really got?
Being rich is much more profound it isn't the external validation from objects or pounds,
that isn't where wealth is found,
So, if you see a person with so much money and so many things
And they are sad, and you can't understand why,
That's because the most valuable thing in life is purely something you just cannot buy.

The words I wish were said.

The words I wish were said,
as if I was a kid getting tucked into bed,
With a cuddle and a kiss on top of the forehead,
An adult I have become, with unsaid words,
I'm left feeling numb,
Despite not being told those words very much,
I know them very well,
My words will never be kept silent like they did when I was a kid in-fact those words I will yell,
The words I wish were said they change every single day,
From a `I love you,` `it's not your fault`, to `you're going to be okay,`,
The words we get told as kids,
are the things we grow up to believe,
but just because some may say bad it doesn't mean things,
we will never be able to achieve,
In fact, you may have had a bad start but in a room full of people you can still have one of the most biggest hearts,
Despite all the pain and heartbreak,
your capacity to love has never been affected,
I know words have been unsaid and that feels like it can never be corrected,
We can hear those words as we grow,
From people we may not even yet know,
The people that were meant to love you when you were small,
May of not gave you that adequate love that was unconditional,
But that doesn't mean you'll never be loved at all,
The words I wish were said that would maybe help me fight the demons better in my head,
You may have been in fear and the right words you didn't get to hear,
But it's not your fault, you've done nothing wrong,
You've been incredibly brave and strong,
You were a little kid, with words left unsaid,
But tonight, when you go to bed,
Remember you are not what you're experiencing in your head,
With all the love you give,

You deserve to have a life to receive love and care but more than that,
you deserve the chance to truly live,
The words that were once unsaid,
We begin to learn to say to ourselves instead.

To be loved.

Sometimes I feel like I want to be loved,
Well in fact I feel like that most of the time,
But I just portray a hard exterior and pretend that I'm fine,
I don't need anyone, that's what I always say,
But I can't help but feel like I wish I would have received that one day,
But not just at any time or any place,
I see it as a child, wishing I had a safe space,
To be cradled in someone's arms and protected from any kind of harm,
I feel that kind of loss, while trying to regulate and heal,
But sometimes I guess I can't always help the way that I feel,
How can you feel at loss at something that you have never received,
And now that I'm an adult can it ever really be achieved?
Figuring out how to grow and overcome unmet needs,
I must try and give that to myself I guess,
But it's hard and doesn't make it hurt any less,
That was meant to come from a certain someone and it hadn't done,
So, there's going to be times where I wish that I was small,
To be cradled and loved and for that to be unconditional,
An independent adult is what they see,
But I just don't want to be dependable,
Because If I lean on somebody else,
And then they go, then I will just fall,
So, I can only depend on me,
But sometimes I wish that wasn't the way it had to be,
I always feel bad for feeling this way,
But I need to remind myself these feelings are okay,
It doesn't make me bad,
Just a little sad,
But it's just a basic human need,
that doesn't have anything to do with selfishness and or greed,
I was once a little girl with that love and care that I didn't quite receive,
But little one that doesn't mean it can never be achieved,
It may not be in the way that it should have been,
But one day you will be seen,
And it may come in a different form,

But you will find and meet people who clear the path for you when you have to face a storm,
So, most of time I seem fine,
But I must admit, I do wish I was loved back then a little more sometimes.

·

Stay or go a different way?

If you think recovering from an eating disorder,
Is simply just fixing the relationship with your body and food,
then I can assure you that you are so far from accurate,
If you think it's just being comfortable with being able to drink the last
bit of milk out of the Cereal bowl,
then you're not looking at the disorder as a whole,
As it isn't about making ourselves look more attractive or skinner,
no because looking sick is anorexia's goal,
I understand how it can be so confusing,
as to why recovery can scare us
But believe me being unwell isn't something we are choosing,
How can something be so soothing yet abusing,
I don't want to be trapped; anorexia set me free,
But I'm just too scared to face the world without you,
So please stand by me,
Are you a friend or an enemy?
I can't seem to decide,
A monster in my head,
My hands feel like they're tied,
Every well done, you're doing great.
My pain through food I Can no longer demonstrate,
My feelings on the surface now with nothing to hide behind,
But I'm learning for myself how to be kind,
Anorexia made me numb to the feelings I didn't want to feel,
But as you recover it's like a volcano of emotions you must work
through to heal,
Recovering can feel like abandonment,
as I no longer look sick,
Recover or stay this way?
I can't seem to pick,
Having to be responsible and accountable for your healing,
While desperately struggling with the card's life is dealing,
I wanted to get better, but at the very same time I wanted to get worse,
But it turns me against all that I love,
till anorexia becomes the centre of my universe,
If only I could just feel the fear and do it anyway,

If only I could not have to listen to the agonising words that the illness has to say,
While it gets louder, I do more it gets prouder,
but it will never be satisfied,
Anorexia, a friend or a foe?
I really don't know,
While deep down I know it's an awful manipulative evil disease,
It convinces you that it'll give you the world and it puts you to ease,
So, you settle for its desires,
but with a tiny voice inside of you saying
"Anorexia let me go, let me go please"
I've Never known something more cruel,
With its negotiations and all its calculations,
The teachers were right, I would be using maths most of my life after all.

Unsteady foundations

How can I build any kind of life on unsteady foundations,
When one minute I feel like I'm unstoppable and nothing can touch me,
Having so many great ideas,
then I just destruct suddenly,
Chaos it's all I've known,
It's familiar and I try to step out of my comfort zone
but no matter how hard I try,
I can't lie and say happiness feels comfortable,
As I wait and wonder when it will all fall apart,
I try not to care or get too attached to things,
as I fear they won't last,
But I have too much care and love in my heart,
I heard it once said
`A child weaned on poison considers harm a comfort,`
Which explains why I reply so heavily on pain,
Which makes a life full of happiness and stability hard to maintain,
I wish I could feel love and feel joy without feeling like it's something
that I need to destroy,
My surroundings don't need to be burning,
And this is something that I'm still learning,
That I don't need to just feel warmth from fire anymore,
I can feel warmth that radiates from the sun,
That despite all the ugliness in the world,
there will be glimmer of beauty,
when all is said and done,
Maybe one day, I will let things just be,
I won't fear the future so much, it won't be as scary,
That good things can happen because they just can
That behind it doesn't have to be a despiteful evil plan,
Where good can be good
And bad will be bad,
I don't need to either destroy everything or put the world to right,
I don't need to be nothing or be everything,
Where I don't need to be a superhero, I don't need to go from a 100 to a
zero, Building a life on unsteady foundations, But even the most broken
pieces can be turned into the most beautiful Creations.

Shades of humanity.

We all bleed the same colour,
We all have the same bones,
We all speak from our mouths but just have different tones,
We all have the same body parts,
We all have a beating heart,
We all cry from our eyes,
We all are guilty of telling lies,
We all feel joy, we all feel pain,
All that I'm trying to say,
Is that in the grand scheme of things, we are all just the same,
And I get we are all unique with separate DNA,
But when all is said and done,
We are all just human beings at the end of the day,
Born to be loved and seek human connection,
The things we go through doesn't define who we are,
it certainly is not a reflection,
although the past and how we grow up can affect how we can be,
It isn't a definition of who we are, it most certainly isn't our identity,
Black or white, gay or straight, we are all just the same but that's not
how society operates,
The world is yet to demonstrate,
That black people shouldn't be shot for a crime they didn't even
commit,
Where people liking the same gender isn't something they are ashamed
to admit,
Why do people give less love and more hate in return?
When is society going to learn/
That a difference doesn't mean someone is less than,
Please tell me when will society learn this?
Because this comes at cost,
Many people each year lives get lost,
Simply because of the shame of the colour of their skin,
Or simply because they are confused about who they are within,
No matter the race, the colour of their face,
No matter the gender or sexuality,
When are people going to face the reality,

That we all bleed the same
That we all feel joy, that we all feel pain,
We are all only human after all,
And love, love shouldn't have to be conditional.

unmasking the unseen.

Behind the girl that claims that she doesn't want to get better,
She'd rather stay unwell, is a girl with a much deeper story to tell,
She wants to be loved,
Yet denies herself of her turn,
Who is yet to learn,
love and care doesn't always have to come from worry or concern,
Behind the girl who doesn't want to live,
Is a girl who just doesn't want to be in pain,
Behind the girl who is mean to herself but loves everyone else,
is a girl who doesn't want another individual to feel the same,
Behind the girl who is angry with the world and finds it too scary,
Knows life can be full of beauty,
That life really can be a special thing,
but she's too scared of the pain that it brings,
As it's brought much more heartbreak than it ever has anything else,
Behind the girl that self-destructs,
even when things are going good,
Is a scared little girl who feels so misunderstood,
Behind the tears,
she's been fighting for years,
And just doesn't want to have to fight to survive anymore,
a girl for her age who is so mature,
But she's never got the chance just to be a kid before,
Too many responsibilities she had to face,
With a fear purely her existence takes up way too much space,
Behind the girl who has no hope,
is a girl filled with dreams she feels she'll never be able to reach,
When she's only so young,
yet has loads of life lessons that she could teach,
She doesn't know what better is,
Deep down she's just scared,
she was never prepared for all that she had to go through,
I know there's many people out there like this girl too,
Where you believe you'll only get acceptation through perfection,
Behind the functioning adult, is a child who just wants to be held
And for expressing her feelings she doesn't want to be yelled,

.

Behind all you see, is a girl who just feels like this is all she's bound to be,
I guess what I'm trying to say is,
I never thought I could be loved just by being me.

Whispers in the silence

Anorexia thrives in silence,
While you decided to stay quiet,
In my head formed a riot,
At first, I believed not being listened to or heard was to be a good thing,
After the euphoria comes all the isolation and devastation that the Illness brings,
While you stepped back as you thought your lack of presence would make it go away,
Anorexia held out its hand out to me,
And said look, see, I'm the only one that will stay,
While the noises of anorexia get louder, it only leads to further decline,
But with all my might and despite having little fight,
I wake up and say that I am fine,
Because in the eyes of the professionals,
they only care until you're at death's door,
If you've suffered for years they just say, `come on,
you know what you need to do, we have been here before,`
With little guidance and lack of people reaching out their hand,
Surrounded by trained professionals who yet still didn't quite seem to understand,
That this wasn't a choice,
I didn't ask to hear the anorexia's voice,
Yes, I know it's me that is listening,
But try to look at anorexia as an abuser who is belittling,
Yes, anorexia is something you cannot see,
But please do not blame me,
Because it's there each day in my mind,
Saying things that are far from kind,
If it was as simple as to just go and eat,
Then more and more people will fight this illness,
this illness they will beat,
But how many people does it take,
Many more people accept defeat,
It's more complicated, devastating than you'll ever be able to know,
While professionals stay silent,
as people aren't viewed as unwell enough yet,

it just leaves room for the anorexia to grow,
Why do we need to let it get to the point where the illness shows
`You're not unwell enough come back later`,
Then `your too unwell to engage` and your left feeling much more deflater
Anorexia isn't a friend, but I can't pretend that I don't use anorexia to lean on as a way to cope,
But while the system lets down so many,
A change to happen is all I can hope,
As I hope many don't fall beneath the cracks,
ending in a slippery slope,
Anorexia thrives in silence,
It crawls it's way in,
just like poison ivy attached to my skin,
I am not just a typical anorexic,
deep down I'm just a lost wanting to be loved within,
It's not just about food or weight,
There's no such thing as sick enough,
Anorexia will not stop, no it will not stop until it's too late.

Tangled emotions.

When i feel any positive emotion,
it feels as if I am flying,
But when it comes to any other negative emotion,
it feels like I am dying,
Because sadness feels like so much more than just being down,
It feels like I have an anchor i have attached to me,
while I'm fighting to stay above water, so that I don't drown,
Happiness feels like I'm unstoppable,
No, nothing can hurt me, no, nothing could hurt me at all,
As I think to myself,
this is what it feels like to be alive,
But minutes later, I can barely survive,
Distance feels like abandonment,
A simple change of tone,
a simple look,
a simple stare,
Thoughts in my head,
thinking they no longer care,
A missed phone call,
or even just a late reply,
I did something wrong,
they hate me and so do I,
Normal feels like nothing, like an empty hole I need to fill,
But from burning, I feel warmth,
From concern, I felt love,
So, tell me when I feel those things,
How am I meant to heal?
When my thoughts are always either, black or white,
And not knowing, which is right,
How do I know what thoughts are coming from me
And how do you know it's not just from my bpd?
My feelings can change as quick as my heart can beat,
One minute, I have so much hope,
the next minute, I accept defeat,
Love feels like your whole,
Heartbreak feels like your a completely lost soul,

Emotions being too much to bear,
I'm just a human being with so much care,
But when I feel anger, I feel rage,
Fury inside of me takes centre stage,
I am not a monster,
In fact, I'm just a scared child within,
As if I'm living in a body that has got third degree burns all over my skin,
The slightest touch or movement can make me feel in agony and in pain,
With everything changing so suddenly,
anything can feel hard to maintain,
I build something to watch myself break it all apart,
I didn't want to, I just felt I needed to,
I just see destruction as art,
You can't create a fulfilling life on unsteady foundations,
How to have any kind of life with society's standards and BPDs expectations?
I don't want to be too much,
I don't want to be not enough,
I want to feel emotions the way that they are meant to be
Sadness just as sad,
And happiness just as being happy,
So when I feel any positive emotions it feels like I'm flying,
But any negative emotions it feels like I am dying,
But please know no matter what I am trying,
To live in a world that felt like it wasn't meant for me,
To live in a world with BPD.

Words left unsaid.

There's no excuse for all the things that I did,
No reasonings, you were just a little kid,
There are no justifications or explanations that I'll be ever able to give,
I robbed you of a childhood leaving you to learn how to survive rather than live,
There is nothing I can say that'll ever be able to take the pain away,
I caused you to be broken, now the only person who can fix you is you
I'm so sorry for all the things I put you through,
You deserved to be loved and held,
I'm sorry because you did nothing wrong, it wasn't your fault
I should not have yelled,
I'm sorry because my apology will never be enough,
But darling, know that you were and are enough,
I should have been the example of who to be
You shouldn't have to fight through life fearing to become me,
I should be your hero, not a person that you fear,
Whenever you're scared you'll run up to me and hug me as I'll say I'm here, I'm right here.
I lost the right of being a parent a long time ago,
Ever since you had to walk this scary life solo,
All I could do was hope I did a good enough job you'd want me in your life as an adult,
But unfortunately because of my actions I don't have you now as a result
It's not your fault and you are not to blame,
You should be so proud of the person that you have became
Breaking generational trauma,
I should have done the same,
You needed to be safe, not strong,
You were a child, and my actions were wrong,
Your past hurt, your future is bright
Don't let the darkness I caused you to dampen your light,
You were a kid, you were small you did nothing wrong,
no nothing wrong at all, You're safe now and you're okay,
These are just some of the unexpressed words that I wished my parents would one day say.

Silent battles

People always say well there are no words you can give,
That will make a suicidal person want to live,
Which some people may believe to be true but I like to see it from a
different point of view,
It isn't just about dying or leaving this earth,
It's a mental illness that impacts your thoughts opinions and you're
worth,
All we want to do is to end the pain,
No matter how hard we try,
We can't articulate or find the words to explain,
what is going on inside our brains,
I always thought it would take something so powerful for someone to
say,
That could make me consider the thought to stay,
Until one day something much more powerful happened,
They didn't need to say anything grand,
They didn't even need to fully understand,
But they were just there, they just held onto my hand,
They listened to me,
when I wanted to give up desperately,
and I know they couldn't change how I felt inside
But they could listen and sit with me while I cried,
when the thoughts felt to over powering I felt terrified,
when I felt my only option left was to choose suicide,
They didn't see me as if I'm unfixable as if I'm broken into a million
parts,
They just knew I was only human with feelings
A human with a beating heart,
Who thought the only way for the pain to stop was for the heart to stop
beating as-well,
With every smile and every mask
Completing everyday and each and every task,
What I was going through no one could tell,
The times I stayed silent when inside my head felt violent and all I
wanted to do was yell,
So people always say there are no words you can give,

to make a suicidal person want to live,
So I was left with no confidence or hope with people saying well if someone wants to die then they just will,
Which leaves me with guilt as my feelings are real,
yet I'm alive still.
But with empathy and an listening ear,
That can just be the very simple but powerful reason as to why a person is still here.

Broken roots to blooming hearts.

Maybe for every reason you don't believe you're worthy of love or care
Is a reason as to why you are,
Which may not make any sense to you,
But I'm just trying to change your point of view,
Because maybe you don't believe you deserve love or care
simply because you haven't received the right amount or the right
definition of it before,
You look for less when in fact you deserve so much more
You feel lonely, scared and insecure
You feel that you are not worthy of love,
You feel so much, even more than the few adjectives that I've just stated
above.
Love and care is a human imperative,
And I'm so sorry if in your life you haven't received that so far,
but it doesn't always have to be the narrative,
Maybe for all the reasons you feel broken is not because of you,
But because of the things you've been through,
Maybe love is a little bit like nutrition,
Lack of it starts to affect your cognition,
You were deprived of the simple things
Those little things that may seem like nothing,
But the things that keeps us as humans alive,
And that's damaged your core beliefs,
And in a way now your having to deal with a kind of grief,
You act the way you do because it's what you feel or what you've been
brought up to believe you deserve,
You hold on to self destruction and self sabotage because at one point in
life it felt like a purpose that would serve,
Something good could come along but you set it on fire,
While you sit and watch and it's now all burnt,
As that's what you learnt,
Deep down care and love is what you desire,
As much as it feels like the only thing to do
I hope you learn to put the matches down beside you,
As maybe things start to look different,
But once where there was what you thought were damaged roots

Flowers then grew,
maybe for all the reasons you feel like you don't deserve love or care is
every reason why you need it more,
To receive that right adequate care, you may have never received
before.
For every reason you don't believe you deserve love or care
Is the exact reason as to why you are.

Rebuilding trust

I'm sorry because I know you are not the issue,
The people that have hurt me are,
I get so scared so I push you far,
Whenever I perceive threat, I hid away,
Resulting into me finding comfort and things that make me feel safe,
that make me feel okay,
I'm sorry as I never give you the chance for you to prove me otherwise,
For you not to act the same way then other people in my life have would
be for me a complete surprise,
I may lash out in ways that seem strange,
But please know I'm trying, it's just so hard to change,
Because of everything I've been through, I have a voice inside my
head,
That makes me believe the world and everyone is against me
So I hide away in bed,
I don't believe I'm loveable, no I don't believe that at all,
In fact I make it hard for people to love me,
I guess I just shut it away as I never believe it could ever be a
possibility,
I get told I'm more than an illness,
I'm a human being with a personality,
It's hard because I live in my mentality but you see the reality
But I don't,
I don't see what you see, so please try, try to be easy,
I'm sorry if I cut you when you are not to blame for my pain,
I'm sorry I'm so quick to judge that you will just be the same
Because it isn't fair and I know deep down in my heart,
you're not, I guess I'm just used to being let down a lot,
But as I go to isolate you say to me you'll wait,
As I walk back and you stand,
Holding and positioning next to the wall I built waiting for me to reach
out my hand
And I can't understand, Why are you waiting?
But you are just demonstrating
The meaning behind the word unconditional
You're not the issue the people that have hurt me are.

The inner light

I'm sorry because you are not to blame, not even a little bit, not at all.
I know you may feel like you are nothing but to someone else you
maybe everything,
Because in reality the thoughts you are having are not you,
And not everything you are thinking is true,
Yes sometimes we can know ourselves more than anyone
But sometimes other people get the chance to see us from a different
perspective,
We can only see a fracture of our true self when all is said and done
You can't see that smile on your face and your face being bright,
You can't see the strength others see when you feel defeat but instead
you fight,
You have these voices and demons all inside of your head,
So strong, so powerful you can't see anything else instead,
When you walk in a room, You don't feel the warmth you radiate,
Despite what you go through you always give a helping hand to others
despite all the things that you have on your own plate.
You may feel that no one wants you around,
But I promise you that it isn't true
You're just feeling lost but that doesn't mean you will never be found,
We never know what simply just our existence can bring and that is the
thing,
You may not be doing anything grand,
And when someone says they want to you stay,
you may not understand,
But I know you may feel like nothing but to someone else you're
everything
And the a world without you would rip them apart
And that isn't a guilt trip just the sad reality
From losing a soul like you someone who has one of the biggest hearts
So please, if you do one thing today,
Let it be you stay,
To hold on, Stay strong, It may feel wrong
But it's right, It hurts at the moment
But existing won't always be a fight
You are loved more than anyone will ever be able to explain,

You are loved because of who you are
You are not your pain.

Creating a home from love.

You've made a home in the pain
And I know this because I have done the exact same,
A home to keep you warm,
A home, a safe space that protects you from the storm
Well at least that's what we think
Until it gets too much and we start to sink,
Where chaos feels much more comfortable than peace,
which is fine till the loneliness and isolation then starts to increase,
If self destruction was a competition,
a gold medal you would achieve
It is not your fault adequate care and love you didn't receive,
I know it feels like just you against your head,
You can't see a way out you can only see darkness and a very long fight
to face instead,
But it isn't your fault I hope that you know,
It isn't your fault you're finding it hard to let go,
Of behaviours or ways to cope,
But just because you can't remember a life without it doesn't mean that
there is no hope,
There will be times where you laugh, times where you'll cry, times
you'll fail no matter how hard you try,
Times you fall, times you'll stand tall
There will be times you'll want to scream,
And there will be times you will feel like you're living in a dream,
The home of pain felt safe to you it's what you knew,
We imagine what it would be like outside of that we may imagine things
that won't be true,
But one things for certain there will always be someone walking beside
you,
that being Your younger self.
Being unwell isn't your identity it isn't all you'll be,
Your home maybe set alight but I promise stepping out you'll be alright
As you're younger self looks up to you and says
Let's go home, a home built from love.

My irrational rational brain

We always talk about my head being an evil thing,
And I get it as an outsider, all you see is the destruction and devastation
that it brings,
But let me tell you, let me try to explain
I know deep down it brings absolutely nothing but pain,
But we always see anorexia as an evil person inside of our brains
And yes I know that is to be true,
But hopefully I can explain it from my point of view,
It is an illness that doesn't want me to be alive but at the same time it is
a coping mechanism that I believe helped me to survive,
It most certainly is an intruder in my mind,
That says the most unpleasant things that are far from kind but it also
feels like
my logical thoughts and those thoughts come from the same place
But it takes up too much room for anything else there is no space,
Sometimes it doesn't feel like an evil monster sometimes it just feels
just like me,
It's an intense impulse and I just want to be free,
How do I stop when it feels like it's coming from a part where my
logical thinking is meant to be,
To you it may not seem logical,
Maybe not even a little bit or not at even all
So yes to a degree it is an evil voice,
But it's not as simple as just not listening to it,
it isn't a choice, The thoughts can almost feel protective,
Something I shouldn't go against,
Something to me that almost just makes sense,
Till my thoughts spiral out of control,
Till I'm trapped in an illness and I didn't even know,
Planning things out in certain way, what I can or cannot do each and
every day,
Sometimes just feels like my logical thinking part of me,
But an evil monster is all you can see,
How do I tell the difference between thinking it's a good skill and
realising it's an deadly illness that can kill.

How do I learn to go against a thing I thought was keeping me safe when in reality all along it was just making me ill.

Be a child, be wild.

I know there's days where you don't want to fight,
You know you need to heal your inner child but you can't even tell
yourself things will be alright,
There will always be a little kid inside, who is kind of surprised you still
feel this way,
Because as a little kid there was a glimmer of hope,
Little you believed there was a chance it could all be okay,
And I know there's some days your not even sure you can live,
And there are some days you can't show up to the world and there's
only so many excuses that you can give,
So many dreams you used to have, you promised you'd make real one
day,
Growing older, it gets harder,
But although you can't see it, there are so many little but beautiful
things that makes it worth to stay,
Yes some days are going to be hard to get through,
But maybe it's not even for you,
But for that little kid you once knew,
Waiting for the tooth fairy or Santa on Christmas Eve,
Or the pure innocence or not knowing what it's like to grieve,
Staying up late and thinking you were so cool,
Or coming back watching tor favourite show after school,
I know you've experienced a lot and you feel those days are far from
over,
But that little kid deserves some closure,
Be immature, regress and heal the kid you were before,
It wasn't her fault for the way that she was raised,
And for all of her courage and times she was scared, should be praised
No more anger or hatred at yourself,
Just a kid with little hands,
who had to carry way more than she should have way more than what
was planned,
Just a little kid who needed somebody, anybody to understand,
But now they have you,
Try not to be angry at your body or keeping hurting a pure and innocent
soul,

You're not your bad experiences no that isn't what makes you who you are as a whole,

Little you is standing in front as you both lock eye to eye,

`Come on`, says little you let's go, let's go give this one more try,

The world felt on top of us, little did we know we had the world right our feet,

That we may have lost so much already but so much more we're yet to meet,

So stay, Because it may not mean much to you but for the little version walking beside who's been there through every tear that you have cried, who wants you both to finally be okay,

to you it may not mean much,

But once upon a time it meant everything to that child,

So go live you life, love and let it be wild,

Go together and chase the sun because the minute you think it's all over it's actually only just begun.

Silenced souls

For a decade of my life, I was looked out for by my parents as a kid,
But for the rest of my time till an adult the NHS did,
I got lost in a corrupt system i was no longer a person,
A place that was meant to heal the experiences of my childhood but in-fact they made it worsen,
for that little me, to be loved and understood she would crave,
She was so scared, she didn't want to be alone she most certainly didn't want to have to be brave,
Fighting against a system that is fundamentally wrong,
Feeling like she's the issue from professionals and her parents,
But little did she know it was never her fault all along,
Why should a little girl have to plead?
And have to fight for a right of basic human need,
From the things she's didn't even break in the first place,
she wanted to heal,
But she was invalidated by you and was told well that isn't how she feels,
She asked for help and help you would decline,
So a smile she would portray and she'd say that she was fine,
She was fighting a battle that no one could see,
Her trauma, her struggles was just labelled as a part of her identity,
Weekly meetings, reviews of prescriptions
In a line, professionals sat on a projector was her description,
Listed with all of her behaviours and trauma and a reminder to why she was brought here in the first place,
Going from a chaotic home, this was meant to be her safe space,
But there was nothing safe about it, no not at all,
No place to call home, just 4 walls in a hospital,
Being treated like an animal in a cage,
They don't all get to know you for you as a person more like from the admission page,
As you open up and say you don't want to live,
A cause for concern you unintentionally give,
And although you have no plans,

In your head you're a prisoner of the things you can't do and all the things you can,
Treatment resistant I may seem to be,
But I'm caught up in a time where no one listened
when I said help me,
In one way or another I've experienced some form of neglect,
so I'm not worthy of many things that's something I detect,
No adequate care from loved ones or even those who are paid
And everyone around me was confused to all my symptoms that I displayed,
With being so self aware they can't understand why I am this way,
Why didn't they listen when I go to say
'Help'?
They let people's behaviours deteriorate and only want to intervene once it's far too late,
For a decade of my life being brought up in chaos and looked out by unavailable parents as a little kid,
then for the rest of my life social care and hospital did,
I must have been the problem, I thought after the way I was constantly treated,
I had no other choice, I was left tired and felt defeated,
Thinking it must have been something that I did wrong,
Little did I know it wasn't my fault,
no it was never my fault all along.

The gap between my thigh.

I know that when the day comes, the day that I die,
There will be no one at my funeral talking about the gap i had In-
between my thighs,
There would be no one discussing all the of things that I ate,
They wouldn't be asking for my final weight,
While they were worried and concerned over my health,
I was proud and happy to hear the word deteriorate,
As that's what anorexia wanted from me,
It wants to suck everything out of you till you have nothing left
And that's just the sad reality,
It wasn't just about wanting to be skinny,
deep down it was about wanting to be loved,
I always thought being loved and cared for was based on kilograms,
I struggled to believe I am worthy and enough just the way that I am,
I wanted to be loved and I really thought I found a friend
but anorexia was nothing but an enemy who lies,
who says i'm the only thing that will have your back
but it's actually all just pretend,
I wanted to be loved as people stand all around,
And the people standing there are the people that love,
the people that care but I was looking for answers and love in something
where those things cannot be found,
I thought there had to be something wrong with me
for that to be achieved,
As much as I hate the life anorexia gives me,
It left to hard to let go of it, I didn't want to grieve,
But by delaying the healing I'm delaying the feeling,
Of what it is deep down that I crave,
To my anorexia I am now just a slave
This isn't the life I wanted to live but I couldn't shut down from all the
false promises the illness gives,
The way it makes me feel euphoric
I didn't think I was unwell,
But why would I have the thoughts I'm having if I wasn't sick?
Validation from your illness will only lead to one thing,

It'll drive you to your death it'll not stop destroying you till you take your final breath,

The amount of energy and effort I put in

Purely because I didn't believe I was worthy or being loved and cared for just by being the person I was within,

it isn't just about food why can't others understand?

It's an addiction that says it has all the answers,

As it reaches out it's hand,

And the more I hold on I believe I'm being strong

but ironically it makes me physically weak,

Till I'm a shell of a person where only anorexia gets to speak,

So no when the day comes the day that I die,

People around won't be talking about the gap between my thigh,

They will be asking themselves why?

Why couldn't I see that what I was convinced the illness could give me they could give me way more

they would be asking why she did she do this to herself for?

The was no rationale for everything that I did,

It was an addiction, it was an illness, it stems from multiple factors from the relationship I have with myself and all the things that I went through as I kid,

If you're going through the same I know your in so much pain,

And I know you feel the world is against you in all you do,

But people are just wishing and praying for you to push through,

Because how you think the world views you isn't the reality,

But it's all well and good knowing that but it's still hard to change our mentality,

Anorexia is an evil destructive disease who will destroy your life with ease,

If you were to listen to one things try to listen to this please,

You can be loved still,

For this to happen you don't have to be Ill,

People's last words about you will never be look what they ate, look at their weight,

It would be describing the soul you were and everything you believed in and all you would demonstrate,

Showing kindness to the world even though your head constantly gave you hate,

.

Please know your worth more than what your illness yells
And to be loved and cared for you don't have to be unwell.

More than one soul

They talk about your younger self as if it's one individual,
but they fail to mention them all,
From when you grew older to the ones when you were very small
As there is more,
Every single year is the person that you were before,
So let's not forget about them,
Instead of talking to your younger self as one soul,
Let's look at all of the versions of you that's made you who you are today as a whole,
We can't just heal one part,
We are so many versions of ourselves with only one heart,
Healing our 8 year old isn't going to put our world to right,
because there was once a 5 year old who needed to be hugged tight
and to be told that everything will be alright,
So imagine you walk into a room/
You're greeted by someone whose eyes are filled with joy,
One individual is listening to music in the corner while another is playing with their favourite toy,
They all put down what they are doing as they come towards you,
These all the people that you used to be,
as you share all the difficult things you've had to go through,
As 8 year old you starts stroking your hair,
3 year old you sitting on your lap letting you know they're there
with 16 year old you looking at you with that certain stare,
As they held your hand and told you they all understand,
And they're proud they just want you to be okay,
That you was enough the way they was and they told you all the things you needed to hear that others didn't say,
You as a baby and your holding them in your arms making sure that they don't come to any kind of harm,
You're surrounded by love despite destroying yourself for many years,
you started to cry as 11 year old you wipes away my tears,
4 year old you, jumping up and down,
7 year old you laughing saying come on where's that smile
your face will stay like that if there weather changes you don't want your face to forever have a frown,

The pure innocence, in a instance all your negative thoughts drown,
13 year old you in the corner who was once filled with loss and devastation,
Comes over and hugs you as they know you were once in broken pieces but somehow you put yourself back together and you've made a beautiful creation,
They are all there with you, every single one,
With love in their heart, passion in their eyes,
They are all so proud of the person you've become,
It's not just about healing one soul,
It's about healing and loving every single part of you as a whole,
Imagine if one day you all could meet,
As your younger self see you standing there as they were going to accept defeat,
But no you stand there tall,
From older version to the version of you when you were small,
And you teach and show them love that unconditional,
they are all standing there and are so happy you are still here
And one day, hopefully not for a very long time yet
Will be older you,
`Look at what we've done dear`
You stayed when you wanted to disappear,
You lived rather then just survived,
All of those versions of yourself are so glad that you are alive,
So never heal one soul,
Heal every part that makes up who you are as a whole

A place where I belong.

From all the rules, restrictions and limitations I just wanted to be free,
I wanted a safe place where I could just be authentically me,
A place where I didn't feel compelled,
A place where I could express my views and opinions as a young person
where someone from higher authority listened to me rather then yelled,
To make friends who are light hearted genuine people where we both
share similar interests, who will love and accept me at my worst and not
only at my best,
A place that I could go to grow,
Where It's safe to be vulnerable and let people know,
The negative emotions at times I have to face,
That it's okay to share because out of everywhere,
this right here is my safe place,
The pressure of the world gets taken away,
A perfect image I don't need to portray,
Because all I have to do is be me and that's good enough,
Because through the dark, the people I found here will be my light,
And I know when I go there everything's going to be alright,
An escape from the outside world,
An escape from all the negativity and limitations and expectations
others have to hold,
Because when I'm here people encourage me no matter what to reach for
gold,
As they cheer me on and they will be my biggest support system
when I find it hard to be strong, At last I finally can breathe because I
finally have a place, a place that I belong,
Home isn't a just building, family isn't just blood,
I built an alternative/ extension to my family and home,
A place and people that I love with all my heart,
A place where I can be different and unique and unapologetically me,
Where no matter what I always will fit in somewhere and will never be
a missing part because when I am there i am not less than anything or
anyone, I am whole,
I may at times lose my way but now I can happily say,
I'm no longer a lost soul,

Creating and building an accepting loving environment is the ultimate goal,
And I'm so lucky to be able to say that's something that I've found,
As I walk into the building the love and compassion radiates all around,
Without this home, this escape, I don't quite know where I'll be, But I don't think about that I just know that I am so lucky,
A place that's safe,
a place that I can just be me,
From Strangers who turned into my friends,
and now my friends who turned into people I now choose to call my family.

Maybe you were just a kid...

Maybe you weren't a terrible person,
Maybe you didn't do anything wrong,
Maybe it was never your fault all along,
Maybe through all these years,
Through All of the fights, through all of the tears,
You were just a little kid learning how to survive,
Waiting for a moment of peace to finally arrive,
Maybe you were angry and maybe you should have been,
Because you shouldn't of had to be an adult even though you were a just teen,
Maybe just because you expressed how you felt doesn't mean you're insane,
Maybe how you felt was valid as what you was experiencing was something that was inhumane,
Maybe what happened wasn't a reflection of you,
Maybe one day you'll realise that actually you were a just human being to,
One day you will learn that love and care you don't have to earn,
That someone can give you affection and protection with not wanting anything back in return,
Maybe you'll realise setting boundaries doesn't make you a bad person,
or putting yourself first isn't anything to do with greed,
As you start to give yourself the basic human needs,
Maybe you were never the problem,
Maybe you got hurt way more than you ever should,
Maybe you were simply just a kid,
Who's past trauma remains in adulthood,
you don't need to punish yourself,
For a crime you've never done,
You were just a kid, you are someone,
Self destructive as an adult as you don't think anyone will care,
It's not as if you don't know what you are doing in fact you are too self aware,
But you can't depend on anyone because who is really going to be there,
But as time goes by and you start to heal,

You know there is such thing as love after all, that it is in fact real,
You were once just a kid please don't punish them or yourself the way
that other people did,
Maybe you're not a bad person in-fact you never were,
Bad things happened, things that should never occur,
Your whole life spent around some sort of violence,
your whole life felt the need to live in silence,
Maybe you weren't a terrible person at all,
Maybe you were just a kid,
And no one should have to carry the burdens you had to when you were
so small,
I'm sorry for the way that you were treated,
I'm sorry because the word sorry won't ever come from the people you
want it to,
Just know if you're going to hate or blame anyone don't let it be you,
Actually There is no maybe about it
You were never the problem, you were just a kid.

My lilac star

You knocked on my door and then turned on my light,
I opened my eyes and said, is everything alright?
I saw the look on your face and my heart immediately dropped,
And it was in that moment everything suddenly stopped,
You told me her name and said that she was gone,
Don't say that, take that back your lying to me I tell you,
you've got it all wrong,
I didn't sleep at all that night and for days after that too
I lost a friend,
I couldn't stop saying the words 'I love you'
To the people that in my life and those that were near,
Because the very person I should have said it more to was no longer
here,
No longer able to deal with the demons in her head,
I was left questioning why she was gone and why it wasn't me instead,
I never thought I would lose a friend so young,
What's even more sadder is she must of thought no one would care
but she doesn't know the sadness and devastation it's brung,
It'll forever destroy me that she did what she did,
But this isn't about me, I'm now an adult and she'll forever be a kid,
Grieving the loss of her, Grieving for all she could be achieving,
She gave out so much love and care,
and more she should have been receiving,
I wish I could have been there by her side,
She must have been absolutely terrified,
To feel like the only option that she had left was suicide,
I still think about her to this day she'll never fade away,
From my mind or from my heart,
I'll forever love and miss her everyday that we are apart,
I thought Id hear your name for so many more years to come,
or i would see your name on my phone when you would of messaged or
rung,
It'll forever hurt me that we lost her so young,
I remember my last hug with her and wished I would of hugged her a
little tighter,
Telling her the heaviest thoughts

She feeling is one day going to start to become more lighter,
It doesn't matter how much time goes by,
I will still sit there asking myself why?
Why you had to go so soon
I look for you in everything I see beautiful sunsets and when it gets to noon,
I look for the brightest star,
As I look up to high in the sky and smile and think to myself there you are,
In my heart my love for you will always have so much room,
I wish we could of all seen that amazing smile and amazing personality bloom,
I will always try and help people the way that you did,
So don't you worry you just rest up now kid.

Borderline

I told you I wasn't fine but you didn't believe a word I had to say your reply was simply 'your just a typical borderline'
As if attention seeking is just a symptom and we should just be ignored,
You gave me a label that's just who I was,
But really I was a person with a lot of trauma and pain that needed to be explored,
No this is more than just a personality trait,
It can stem from invalidation and neglect,
But that's exactly how the mental health system operates,
By providing the same thing that caused the BPD in the first place,
Rather than treating us like humans who need to be heard and believed, and given a little extra love and care,
you treat us like we are just this hopeless pointless case,
And you just prove that it doesn't matter about speaking out because no one's going to be there
This is just the way they will be,
don't feed into their thoughts or they mentality,
It will only make them pay attention to it more,
it'll only make the thoughts worsen,
Maybe I do want love care and attention but since when doesn't make me such a bad person,
Sorry I had got brought up to believe love and care isn't something you just receive,
I know I act in extreme ways that seem irrational,
but when I feel something inside I want to scream I want to hide because I feel it all,
I may have BPD but I am not a monster or a narcissist
everyone with bpd isn't the same
Most of us aren't manipulative violent people
We are just young kids who weren't taught how to properly handle our emotions and our pain,
Please don't look at me and just see a monster within,
I am not a monster, I'm a human with blood bone and skin
But I do have a monster in my mind but that doesn't make a horrible person or unkind,
But what you'll find is I am black and white

One minute I'm in the pits of disappear the next I'm alright,
And I'm not making it up I'm not insane,
I just feel things in extreme,
me and you just don't think or feel the same,
I'm so sorry for the way that I can be,
I wish my head didn't make me feel this way,
I wish I could live in a world without BPD,
Fear of abandonment, fear people will leave
On top form one minute life couldn't get any better
the next I'm left unable to breathe,
Clingy one minute, then pushing you away the next,
I'm sorry I jump to conclusions and take things way out of context,
Please know it's isn't all I'm defined by,
I act in ways I sometimes don't know why,
I'm trying to regulate and heal,
I don't need you to fix me just listen to how I feel,
validation and patience is key,
I am way more than my BPD.

Life's beautiful little things

It's the littlest of things that can make life so beautiful,
As much as there's so much hatred and devastation
And many things in this world that people may destroy,
If we all just take a moment and look around we will find there can
actually be so much joy,
In many things we may have never noticed before,
We will never ever run out of these things as we'll always discover
many more,
There can be beauty found in the things that we create,
It could be by nature, which then we turn it into art,
But there can be such profound beauty inside all of us,
All it takes is having a good heart,
And that's something everyone is capable of having,
Like when a random stranger smiles at you in the street,
Or there's this person you just feel safe with as soon as you meet,
Or when you don't feel like you're doing a good enough job
but someone looks at you and tells you that they're proud of you,
Or seeing someone else who's been in the darkness for so long
who lost hope who's light starts shining through,
How we all sing a song to celebrate someone being alive another year,
Or how we all come to together as British people when sweet Caroline
we begin to hear,
Sometimes we can laugh so hard we even begin to cry,
When we are nervous or excited we can get butterflies in our tummies
without even knowing why,
Beauty in seeing all of the sunrises and all of the sunsets,
Life is about making memories rather than living in a lifetime in regret,
Life can be a very difficult thing,
But we never know what each chapter could bring,
How as humans we like to watch our breathe float away in the cold air,
The feeling we get after finding someone who genuinely cares
Or laying in the park looking up high,
Calling out what the clouds look like and what they've formed into in
the sky,
Seeing an excited child loving something that you used to as well,

Or looking forward to seeing your friend and telling them all the funny stories you just have to tell,
Knowing we all have a inner child within,
That we are all only human in bones and skin,
That feeling we get when we get nostalgia from the things we used to do as a kid,
When we were small and didn't over think everything that we did,
Or how we all look out the window when it's snowing in amaze as if we've never seen it before,
The beauty is found in the things that matter to us deep to the core,
The things that make us smile the things that bring us laughter the things that are meaningful and pure,
Life can get in the way,
And sometimes the world is full of so much darkness we question if we are ever going to be okay,
But the sun is always there even at times we cannot see,
In autumn time it teaches us the beauty of letting go when we see the leaves fall from the tree,
There will always be something in this life that'll make life worth living,
There's beauty in receiving but also in giving,
Bad thoughts and feelings are temporary,
We will never know in the next moment what we will feel,
But what we do know is sometimes it takes time to heal,
We all get wounded and yes some may clear up while others remain,
But in time you'll be able to acknowledge it and it maybe a part of you but it doesn't cause any pain,
Beauty can be found in things we can't quite explain,
Someone once said to me life gets better make sure your there to see it
Even if you have to take it bit by bit,
Minute by minute,
Day by day,
Because every sky that is blue was once grey,
It's the littlest of things that make life so beautiful,
And your existence plays a massive part,
Purely from The beauty from your soul and from your heart,
So I hope you take a moment as you look round to see,

.

That yes life is filled with pain and misery but there's also lots of beauty.

The whirlwind of my mind

When you hear the words ADHD,
In your mind all you see is a little boy,
Who's ever so naughty,
You think ADHD is just being lazy,
You think it's someone who just gets high energy out bursts who seems as if they're completely and utterly crazy,
But please let me try to explain,
What really goes on in someone's ADHD brain,
Firstly my mind feels active 24/7 every single day,
My mind is so busy,
which leads to poor time management, which means plans I then delay,
But I can assure you I don't mean to be this way,
I may forget all the information you have just told me,
As in my head I think about all I haven't done and all I have left to do,
my lack of focus doesn't mean I'm being rude if it seems like I'm not listening to you,
But not only that I get distracted by songs and sounds inside my head,
or coming up with big impulsive ideas when I have so much other things to do instead,
this constant noise,
Makes me shut down and I feel so tired I almost feel paralysed in my bed,
My focus is nowhere yet everywhere,
I could have a random sudden interest in a random hobby,
then the next minute I no longer care,
There's something that I go to do,
But then I remember all the other things that I have to do too,
So i stop that for a minute and say i'll come back,
but I started a completely different task now and have gone completely off track,
Having ADHD isn't just about being hyper and having so much energy,
And as much as it's nothing to be ashamed of having,
Having it isn't quirky,
Information will come in my mind then quickly go,
There's so many things I have to face that others don't even know,
My mind is so fast but my body is so slow,

As I then start to procrastinate,
Feeling like a failure,
As I have so much to do but I always leave it till it's too late,
My lack of focus and concentration,
Makes it so hard to operate,
The simple of daily task of life's can take me hours to actually do,
But I know it's important and it's never actually because I don't want to,
It makes me feel like a failure and effects myself self-esteem,
So no ADHD isn't just about being hyper it's much more extreme,
So you may get frustrated with the parts that are caused by my ADHD but please try to know and understand there is so much more to me.

Embracing the spectrum.

I wouldn't change you for the world,
But I wish I could change the world for you,
You aren't any less, you just have a different thought process,
and just see the world from a different point of view,
I want for you to be able to stim how every much you wish,
And although I can't change the worlds entire opinion on autism,
I just want you to know this,
To never change who you are or feel the need to mask,
To know I'm ever so proud of you as I know things can be so
overwhelming,
even if people see them as such a simple task,
If the lights are too bright,
the music is too loud,
If your getting to anxious as you're in a big crowd,
Some things I may not be able to change,
But what I can,
I promise to rearrange,
because I wouldn't change you for the world but I would change the
world for you,
Your autism doesn't mean the things that others achieve you can't do
the same,
I'm so sorry that you get questioned for being yourself you shouldn't
have to explain,
Autism isn't a shame it is just a name,
to describe how your mind processes things,
Autism doesn't mean you won't experience all the exciting things life
can bring,
If the light too bright then the light we can dim,
Your nervous your excited you go ahead and stim,
Be who you are not what you think others expect you to be,
Be your authentic self because it's honestly a beautiful sight to see,
I wouldn't change you for the world but I would change the world for
you,
All I want is for you to be happy.

The journey within

Have we ever thought about what it's like to be a human being for a just second,
Where we don't strive for perfection,
And our value isn't based on our reflection,
And that we are all just souls who seek and need deep connections,
We work so hard to be good enough,
in this world we never chose to be in,
We concentrate on all the imperfections on our skin,
That we forget what holds the most beauty and power is the person we within,
That getting annoyed at something doesn't make us bad,
That we can still be worth something and won't be a burden even if we are sad,
As humans we will experience all kind of emotions,
All the good and all the bad are all okay to feel,
That no matter how much time goes by,
Each day we are alive we have lots to learn still,
It's okay there is no rush take your time to heal,
That making mistakes doesn't have to be a bad thing,
Because think of all the lessons that it brings,
We are bound to get hurt as human species on this universe,
But hurting and being hard on ourselves will only make it 100 times worse,
Your aloud to take a break when life feels too heavy and too much to bare,
That you are enough and have made a difference to someone's life without even being aware,
As humans we get to love, we get to care and that can be beautiful thing to give and receive,
What we also need to remember is many times we may fail before we start to achieve,
But that doesn't mean we give up,
No we keep going,

As humans we wake up and get on without knowing what the future has to hold,
We set our self limitations based on opinions others have told,
But we get to be whoever we want to be,
we get to change the narrative of our story and nobody will ever be able to write our reality,
As humans we will get things wrong,
Some days will test us and make us question if we are even able to carry on,
But as a human being embrace anything that comes your way,
And know your only human, you're okay,
You're more than enough and don't need to strive for more,
We get to be loads of different versions of ourselves
as we grow we learn from the person we were before,
We are going to think and feel bad things at times
But that isn't a crime,
We are only human after all,
And no matter what we deserve to give ourselves love that is unconditional,
You may not be able to make the world better,
But you make someone's world better just by being who you are,
And whenever you think you haven't achieved much,
Just look behind you and see how you've come so far,
Please don't punish yourself for things that are out of your control,
You may feel broken but you will one day become whole,
It's okay to want to be loved for yourself instead of it just being something you constantly give,
I hope there's a day where you look back on all you've done and be able to say I've done it I've truly lived,
Be whoever you want to be,
see whoever you want to see
Let people judge, comment or stare,
Because in a world full of hate and devastation there will always be a corner filled with love and care,
And right now that may feel like something you'll never find,
But as humans in a world where we can be anything let's choose to be kind,

.

We are all brought into this world we never choose to be in but what we need to remember is,
What holds the most power and beauty is who we are within.

The journey among shadows.

I told people I didn't want to get better,
But one day someone once looked at me and said no I think you do
I then pleaded and said no you don't understand I promise everything
I'm telling you is true,
I said the words I don't want to be alive,
And somebody said no it isn't that you just don't want to have to
survive,
Normally everyone would just listen and not sure what to say the words
they couldn't find,
When i tell them those kind of thoughts that are going on in my mind,
But no one till that day said anything like I don't think that's true
before,
And I wanted to scream from my core and cry because I couldn't
understand why they were saying those words when I stated clearly I
didn't want to be here anymore,
But after time I figured actually they were right,
That it's not that I don't want happiness it's just I'm stuck in the
darkness and can't see there being any chance of it becoming bright,
I didn't want to die but I didn't want to live in a world that just feels like
it never gets better no matter how many chances and opportunities I
give,
I didn't want to isolate myself and have no one around,
When I said those words it's also saying I feel so lost and don't think I
can be found,
I didn't believe I brought any kind of value to this universe,
And what makes it worse is I didn't think other people thought I did
too.
I don't want to do this anymore also means I'm scared of this pain,
I'm tired of having to go through the same each and every day,
I'm tired of pushing people away when all I actually want is for them to
stay,
I don't want to get better also means I'm scared about how that might
look,
Because all we think about is seeing it as a coping mechanism,
sometimes view it as our whole world forgetting everything it destroyed
and everything mental illness took,

So I said I didn't want to get better and someone said no I think you do,

But it wasn't in an invalidating way because come to think of it it was true,

Of course I would love to live in a world where mental illness isn't all I'd be,

If only I didn't need to question what I would be like without it as now it's feels like a part of my identity,

When someone says they don't want to be alive anymore is that what they're really saying,

When deep down that individual is just praying the pain become over,

They just want closure from the demons they have to face,

They don't want to live this in a dissociative state as if they're viewing the world from outer space,

As much as I mean the words I say and feel,

I may say I don't want to get better when deep down the very thing I want to do is heal,

I may say I don't want to be alive when really all it is,

I don't think I can take another day where I barely just survive,

When I tell you the words I think I want to die,

That's because I don't think anyone will care if they have to say goodbye,

Words have so much more meaning behind,

When someone's opening up just listen and be kind

and know there's probably more behind the words that they say,

They don't need you to do much just give them a smile then give them a hug as you tell them you're going to be okay,

even when they don't see it that way,

Because in a minute you where they may have being feeling thoughts of suicide,

Your love and care and kindness can be powerful enough for them, disbursing thoughts to subside,

Just try your best to understand, hold our hand,

And know we are so much more than the feeling we describe.

Messages of hope.

Written by friends and important people in my life, and
people who contributed through social media who I've
never even met to show you're not alone, there is hope
and you're loved no matter what!

Life isn't always easy but the pockets of peace and happiness you will feel one day will be worth all the pain,I promise.

The sun is shining brightly behind the clouds, enjoy the nights when the stars glow and wait for the sky to clear, everything will be okay <3

you can't go back and change the beginning but you can start where you are and change the ending"- C.S Lewis

Just stay you. The best thing is just to stay you! With love, with passion, with Hope ,with peace. Patience is always the key

"There are moment that will test you and moments that will treat you but never forget that "Everything happens for a reason, at the exact moment it happens, even if it doesn't make sense at the time I promise you one day you will look back and it will!" Believe in yourself and you are halfway there!

If hope is all you have, you have enough.

We are all struggling but we can get through it together because we are strong and you just need to believe in yourself because you are amazing

Hope is there -grab a chair, talk and share your despair.

take a deep breath.
just stop to slowly inhale and exhale, breathe with purpose. feel your
chest rise and fall. no matter what today did or didn't do, keep breathing.
keep breathing for all the days you're yet to experience and fall in love
with. keep breathing for all the sunrises and pictures of the sky.
keep breathing for yourself and all of the incredible things you are
destined to accomplish. healing is scary, and recovery can be daunting,
but nothing will ever compare to the moment you look back and say "¡
made it". heal for you, recover because you are stronger than your past
and keep breathing through it all.
all my love
Juliette

We have all had days where life is a struggle
Perhaps people have let us down
Or we lose a loved one or are anxious
Thoughts in our head can overwhelm us
And we can feel disconnected with ourselves and others
However I believe and know from experience that it is possible to relax
away those thoughts that upset us
The more we relax those thoughts by either relaxation or meditation or
whatever works for you , the happier you will be
Once I was sad and overwhelmed
Now I'm happy! You can be too
You are so much more than those thoughts
You are the laughter and joy and peace when those thoughts are
clogging your brain

"To anyone going through a tough time, please remember when you
feel like you have nothing left, you can always have hope. Hope that
things will get better. Keep fighting for the future you deserve, recovery
is possible"

Ive been stuck in the dark before but I promise eventually there will be light. You just have to keep pushing forward and searching for the light if you are feeling like you've hit rock bottom, or maybe that feeling is yet to come, just know that the pain will pass. It will be a long journey with different shaped bumps along the way, some good some bad, but that journey will always lead to happiness. Even if it seems impossible you hold the power to heal, a smile from a stranger, sunlight peeking into your room and the sound of laughter are all proof that not all the light is gone and that hope will always be by your side, no matter how alone you feel. Things will get better.

When I googled what hope meant it said "a feeling of expectation and desire for a particular thing to happen" however I disagree. I think hope is more of a grasp on what life will be. There is an expectation that with hope you can achieve anything, but I think hope is more putting the candles in the cake than lighting them. Hope is I know they are there. All I have to do is light them, when I light them, they will glow so beautifully, and I can see that I have lit them myself. Let people hand you the matches, let people see the hope in your eyes and let them help you to get one step closer to that glow. I think the beauty of hope is that it never runs out, you can blow the candles out and keep relighting them. We know that other people can blow them out, you can blow them out yourself but hope is knowing that you can relight them. Knowing. One last final thing, just because you were born into a burning building, it doesn't mean that the world is on fire. You're not responsible to put that fire out, you deserve your small corner of the earth that is peaceful and flame resistant.

As someone who has suffered from anxiety since early childhood, it is a particularly horrible disease. It affects a person mentally and physically. An onlooker does not see the anxiety within a person, they think what a very outgoing, confident person. If it were a broken leg, or a bad bruise, they can see it. Having said all that, there are many things a sufferer can do. For example, talk, talk about it.
Try to live in the moment.
I say to myself, worrying, will not help the situation, it will not help the outcome in any way. Above all, try not to give up hope. It is very much a day to day thing. A good cry, when you are on your own, in my opinion, also helps very much. Remember, you are not on your own. It is very true, in these times, many many more people suffer from it. Also, there is a better understanding of it. So you try to remember, you are not on your own, try to get out every day, and never lose hope.

I have suffered with mental illnesses for over a decade. I never believed in "hope" or that things would get better and every time things got better something worse would happen. I was told a quote by someone which said "if not today, try tomorrow, just never give up, you are enough". That stuck with me for years. Through all my battles I faced I got back up, dusted myself off and tried again. Things were really tough. I had to reach truly rock bottom to believe I had a life worth living. I deserved to enjoy good things, I deserve to be happy, to live a life, to experience freedom away from this dungeon I was living in. Block those people, ignore toxicity, remove harm, embrace love, light and wholeheartedness.
There is never a right time to pick yourself up, and open your eyes to the world of good and compassion and love and joy in a chaotic world we live in today. One day you will wake up and you'll choose this is how you want to live. What I say is don't force it to happen but just let it be. It'll come. You have to be in a place where you're ready for a lot of change to happen and manifest. It's exhausting. But oh my, it is so so worth it. My darling friends reading this,
There is hope for you, there are people out there who will back you in your corner, there are good, positive uplifting people who will help you support you in your corner. If not today try tomorrow and if not then try

the next time. Just don't give up! Pause, lean on that wall and take a break just don't give up please. There is beauty in life and what you make of it. You'll see the good in the bad and the sun will shine down on you once again. You are amazing, you are worthy, you deserve a life worth living and you are so goddamn enough. Keep going, you'll be an inspiration to someone, someday who will be known as that person who despite their struggles, you never gave up.
And to end my favourite quote "Life is difficult, but you are loved"-
Charlie Mackesy
-    Chey

Life is never easy for anybody, you never know what's going on in their life. You can think they have the perfect life, but there are always things nobody is shown. The last 5 years for myself has been a very difficult one, relying on alcohol and pills to sleep at night. Trying to end my life, but on the outside everyone saw me as a happy jokey person. I had a lot of trauma I was living with, things from my past. I lost my best friend to suicide, I felt like nothing was ever going to get better, But I was lucky enough to have people in my life who I finally opened up to. It took me a couple years to finally talk about everything but they have been nothing but supportive. I just wish I opened up sooner. I still think about her all the time, and it still hurts so much, but I try to appreciate the time I had with her, even if it wasn't for as long as I wanted. I'm not one to talk about my feelings to anybody, but I don't know what I would do without the people who pulled me out of the dark. What I'm trying to say is no matter how much you think things can't get better, they can. You just need to realise you have people in your life who will be there and want you in their life. I'm so grateful I was pulled from the dark, I would have missed so many milestones with my nieces and nephew. Missed out on meeting the most amazing people, creating once in a lifetime opportunities. Suicide is never the answer, you may lost the pain your feeling, but it passes it onto so many others. It took me a long time to come to that conclusion. I would be lying if I said there were days I didn't think negative thoughts, but you have one life. It makes you a much stronger person. You just need to hold on, things will get better, even at the worst of times. You're loved. You're wanted. Life wouldn't be the same without you in it. You're amazing, you just need to realise your worth

If you're seeing this and thinking about ending it all, please read this message first.

You hear people saying their inbox is open and they're only a message away, but I also know you don't believe them. You feel like a burden and that the world would be better off without you. You might have been failed by the very services that should be protecting you, and you feel so incredibly lonely. I hear you.

You don't have to make huge leaps of progress to be heading in the right direction. It's perfectly alright to take things minute by minute, and if your only goal for today is to stay alive then that's ok too! It doesn't matter if you've not showered in a week, if your house is a mess or if you can't remember the last time you picked up a toothbrush. Getting through the day is what matters.Practically speaking, you could try practising gratitude – bear with me on this one! It doesn't have to be anything major; just one small thing each day that you're proud of or one small good thing that's happened. It could be that you've got clothes to wear, even if they've not been washed in a while. It could be that you kept yourself alive today, or that you have hobbies you'd like to return to in the future. Another thing you could try is splashing cold water on your face, so you feel something other than the numbness of depression. I've found crochet, reading, pets and adult colouring books helpful in the past. It's about distracting your mind just long enough for the worst of these feelings to pass. When you do survive your worst days, you'll have something to be proud of. Social media portrays the 'ideal life' as a house and a car and 2.4 children but that's just not a reality. If today's biggest achievement was continuing to breathe then you should be so proud of yourself. I'm so proud of you. You've got this!

A message of hope from myself to you, words of love for the one who's faced enough, a smile I give to you to show that you can to, a connection through words I give to you, a glimmer of hope when you feel unable to cope, a hand extended to pull you back in, a lifeline a guideline, a connection of pure, to fix that feeling of broken and raw… because you really do deserve a feeling of more and that's why hope is that feeling, the word I want you to feel today a glimmer inside that mind to help you today find your shine

It's because of people like you that I can see the future in colour. People who have fought to stay when everything is dark and grey, holding on to the hope that the world won't always be so dull. Every sketch starts out blank but we will walk through the outline of our world and colour it in, day by day adding a little more light, because you are here and I am here and they are here. Can I tell you a secret? Sometimes I get tired of colouring after a while, but it's okay to rest and hand the crayon to someone else, so that we can return again another time. I love you.

On my darkest days, enduring the most difficult heartbreak and emotion I had ever felt, I always reminded myself: as the sunsets and the day is over, tomorrow promises a new day. Each difficult day that passes and I fight through, I am one day and one sunrise closer to happier times ahead. The most beautiful experiences and memories to be, are soon enough in the near future. So fight through the difficult days, embrace your emotion. But always remember there is sunshine just ahead. Xx

You're enough, always believe in yourself, follow your dreams. L.C

To anyone going through tough times.

Just know that you CAN do this, I fully believe in you and know you will get through this.

Always hold on to hope.

H.O.P.E - Hold On Pain Ends

You 100% deserve recovery, not a single person doesn't, it's about progression not perfection. Remember everyone's journey is different but it's always worth it, remember it's a marathon not a sprint.

Deep breaths bestie, you've got this.

Sending all my love.

Every morning that you wake up you have a choice... choose YOU <3

letting go, of anything, is the one of the hardest things you'll ever have to do and when that thing has kept you feeling safe and comfortable, it feels impossible. But it's not, not one person regrets recovery. Slowly parts of your life will fall back into place and it will all make sense again

I know things seem tough right now, I've been there before. The thoughts are loud and the urges are strong but I want you to know, you are stronger than you realise, you're fighting a battle no one else can see and you're doing it so well. You are perfect the way you are and you are never alone. You may be feeling defeated but you have come this far, you've got through this before and you can do it again. Everyone reading this book is rooting for you, and we are all so proud of you

A stands for awesome

u means unique

t is tremendous

I for incredible

s for super

m is marvellous.

There have been times in my life that have felt impossible to survive. I have wondered if I really was made for this earth and during that time I felt the most lonely. One of the biggest things that helped me was connecting with people and feeling less alone. So I want you to know that you're not alone in this struggle. You can find strength in solidarity in those around you. Your cousin, your neighbour, your childhood friend, someone from your gym, the barista at your favourite coffee shop, the postman. There are people out there who will understand how you feel and sometimes there can be comfort in that. When you're feeling alone and think there is nobody in the world that could understand the pain you feel, remember that I am here, and I stand in solidarity with each of you reading this. There is hope for a better future. There is hope that you will live a life where pain doesn't consume your life. There is hope that you can heal and be a person that you're proud of. Hope is real, that's one of the most beautiful things about it. It can guide you through and heal your heart. It can heal you.

Hope stands for hold on pain ends.

In the darkness of our own mental health when we never see a way out remember these is always one day of hope, one day that we will not be crippled by our struggles but thank them for what they've show us the tears we cry because we just feel like giving up will one days turn into a distant memory instead replayed by genuine smiles, I have suffered with mental illness for as long as I can remember although I still struggle although I still have my bad days but my good days out way so many of my bad now I never saw a way out until a way out was my only option asking for help was once a crime to me until I realised it's okay to struggle and ask for help, but please remember one thing yours story's not over so please keep living because your life has no end chapter.

Whitney Clark.

The odds of you existing and reading these words are 1 in
10^2,685,000. That second number is a 10 followed by 2.7 million
zeros.

00000000000000000000000000000000000000000000000000000000000
00000000000000000000000000000000000000000000000000000000000
00000000000000000000000000000000000000000000000000000000000
00000000000000000000000000000000000000000000000000000000000
00000000000000000000000000000000000000000000000000000000000
000000000000000000000000000000000

Imagine that number of zeros… 2,685 times over.

It's easy to feel insignificant, meaningless even..but don't forget that
every breath you take is a miracle.

You are beautiful and rarer than any gemstone ever imagined.

There's always going to be someone there, someone to listen, someone to care, someone to love you when you feel unable to, Please know, you are not the bad things you're going through x

Reach out to friends or family!

Or

Call Samaritans – 116 123

Text shout on 85285

For LGBTQ + talk to switchboard on 0300 330 0630

.

Call Calm on -0800 58 58 58

Printed in Great Britain
by Amazon